Bringing Lent Home with
Pope Francis

Prayers, Reflections, and
Activities for Families

Donna-Marie Cooper O'Boyle

Ave Maria Press AVE Notre Dame, Indiana

Founded in 1865, Ave Maria Press is a ministry of the United States Province of Holy Cross.

www.avemariapress.com

Paperback: ISBN-13 978-1-59471-617-1

E-book: ISBN-13 978-1-59471-618-8

Cover image © Lisa Maree Williams, Getty Images News.

Cover and text design by Katherine Robinson.

Printed and bound in the United States of America.

Lovingly, for my children:

Justin,

Chaldea,

Jessica,

Joseph,

and

Mary-Catherine

as well as my grandson, Shepherd

ACKNOWLEDGMENTS

With a grateful heart to my family and friends, especially my parents, Eugene Joseph and Alexandra Mary Cooper; and my brothers and sisters, Alice Jean, Gene, Gary, Barbara, Tim, Michael, and David—I am eternally indebted.

My children—Justin, Chaldea, Jessica, Joseph, and Mary-Catherine—I love you! My husband, David, thank you for your love and continued support of my writing!

Special thanks to Robert Hamma, Thomas Grady, and the wonderful team at Ave Maria Press for their partnership in getting this fourth Lenten book in our series out to you!

INTRODUCTION

Lent is a distinctive, holy season of forty days on our Church's calendar. The number forty is significant. There were many times throughout salvation history when the number forty was important. For now, we focus on the fact that Jesus fasted for forty days in the wilderness. During Lent, we are called to fast, give alms, and pray so the bonds that are holding us back spiritually can be broken and we can grow closer to God.

The season of Lent is meant to transform hearts and souls. In order for true transformations to happen, though, we need to whole-heartedly apply ourselves so that we are not just simply giving up chocolate or some other pleasure for a period time. We should really want to rise to the challenge of these forty days and truly make some extra efforts. The opportunity to do this with your family is an extra blessing.

Pope Francis is an outstanding spiritual guide for your family's Lenten journey. His teachings are simple enough for children to grasp yet his unique background and training as a priest, bishop, and pope and his knowledge of what is necessary to grow in holiness is extensive.

Pope Francis encouraged us in the apostolic exhortation *The Joy of the Gospel* to get to know Jesus better and to allow Jesus to touch our hearts. He specifically said, "I invite all of you who follow Jesus, wherever you are, to spend time every day renewing your personal relationship with him, letting him touch your hearts" (par. 3). What more perfect time to do this than during Lent?

This book will provide and encourage a daily occurrence of family prayer and communication as you move through this holy season together. By following the suggestions regarding how your family can apply Pope Francis's wisdom to your lives, you will participate more fully with the rhythm of the Church regarding Lenten prayer, fasting, and almsgiving.

You can choose morning or evening to gather with your brood (or hopefully both). Your time will be well spent reflecting on Pope Francis's life and wisdom, as well as the great traditions of Holy Mother Church.

To use this book, simply gather your family and move page-by-page, day-by-day, forging your way through Lent. You can come together at your kitchen table, around a prayer table, or wherever you feel most comfortable when praying as a family in your domestic church. Make it special—light a prayer candle if you wish.

Pope Francis's Inspiration: Each day a quote from Pope Francis begins the page and sets the tone for the Lenten day in your domestic church.

Parent Reflection: You will be given some points to ponder in this section each day. Part of it will be for you and some is for your children. If possible, try to read it in advance of gathering together.

Family Prayer: There are two opportunities for prayer during each day of meditations—one at the beginning and one at the end. Feel free to elaborate and adapt to suit your family's needs.

A Story from Pope Francis's Life: This book will highlight notable parts of Pope Francis's life. This part can be read by an older child or a parent.

Fasting: Each day "fasting" suggestions will be made to help guide you, the parent, and your children about what to fast from. It will not only be from certain foods but more often will be fasting from bad habits or enjoyable activities. Feel free to adapt it to what works best for your family.

Ash Wednesday and Good Friday are days of fasting and abstinence. Church law requires that no meat may be eaten on these days by Catholics fourteen years and older. People with medical conditions, pregnant women, and nursing mothers are exempt from fasting and abstinence. Catholics from the age of eighteen through fifty-nine must fast on these days by only having one full meatless meal and two smaller meatless and penitential meals. The two small meals together should not equal a full meal.

Almsgiving: Each day "almsgiving" suggestions are provided to help with ideas to do as a family or individual.

All through the Day: Each day you will be given a simple yet poignant thought to think and pray about throughout the day.

Pope Francis instructed, "Lent is to adjust life, to fix life, to change life, to draw closer to the Lord."[1] May your family receive many rich blessings and graces as you pray, fast, and give alms together, adjusting and fixing your lives, and journeying toward heaven and its rewards throughout this Lenten season.

The logic of the Cross . . . is not primarily that of suffering and death, but rather that of love and of the gift of self which brings life. . . . Following and accompanying Christ, staying with him, demands "coming out of ourselves," requires us to be outgoing; to come out of ourselves, out of the dreary way of living faith that has become a habit, out of the temptation to withdraw into our own plans, which end by shutting out God's creative action.

—*General Audience, March 27, 2013*

Parent Reflection

Today is a very special day because we are entering our Lenten journey. How fortunate we are to be reminded by our Church that we are embarking on a very exceptional and holy time within the Church cycle in which we can commit ourselves to prayer, fasting, and almsgiving to please God and to grow in holiness! Today, when you call the family together to begin your Lenten observance, explain to the children that we work hard to do three things each day during Lent. First, we give up something, which is called fasting. Second, we give something to others. This can be some sort of help, possessions, or money we share with others. This is called almsgiving. Finally, we pray more. As Catholics, all three of these things should be an ordinary part of our daily lives, but during the season of Lent, we focus on them more intensely.

Ask the children if they have given any thought to *giving up* something for Lent. Or, do they want to *do something* special to please Jesus? Take time today to help them decide what to do and to formulate their Lenten resolutions. You can share with them what you plan to do. Help the children to write down their resolutions. They can refer to their notes each day throughout Lent. You might want to hang them on the refrigerator or their bedroom door, write them on a dry-erase or chalk board, or post them wherever they can be reminded easily. In addition to their general Lenten commitment, daily suggestions will be offered as you move day to day throughout Lent.

The words we will hear today when we receive our ashes, "Remember, you are dust and to dust you will return," should help us realize that we need to turn away from sin and seek what Jesus wants for us. Let us be mindful of Pope Francis's words above throughout our Lenten journey: "Following and accompanying Christ, staying with him, demands 'coming out of ourselves.'"

Let's follow, accompany, and stay with Christ this Lent. He will indeed change our lives!

Family Prayer

All make the Sign of the Cross.

> *Parent*: Dear Jesus, help us to not be dreary Catholics. Open our eyes and our hearts to the Holy Spirit during our Lenten journey. Change our lives!

> Now let us listen to these words of Pope Francis.

A parent or child reads the opening quotation aloud.

> *All*: Blessed Mother Mary, bring us closer to your Son, Jesus.

A Story from Pope Francis's Life

Jorge Mario Bergoglio (Pope Francis) was born on December 17, 1936, in Buenos Aires, Argentina. He is the son of Italian immigrants. His father, Mario, was an accountant who worked for the railways and his mother, Regina Sivori, was exceedingly busy dedicating her time to raising their five children.

Fasting

Today, fast from wanting things to go your way.

Almsgiving

Today, give your heart to God more fully, allowing him to work in you and through you.

Today's Intention: Let's pray to be more attentive to those in need, especially those in our own home.

Closing Prayer: Dear Jesus, please teach us the full message of the Cross.

All pray the Our Father, Hail Mary, and Glory Be.

All through the Day: I want to prepare my heart for God to work in it throughout Lent.

Remain steadfast in the journey of faith, with firm hope in the Lord. This is the secret of our journey! He gives us the courage to swim against the tide. Pay attention . . . to go against the current; this is good for the heart; but we need courage to swim against the tide. Jesus gives us this courage!
—*Homily, Holy Mass of Confirmation, April 28, 2013*

Parent Reflection

How often we parents need to be courageous in our role; parenting is not for the faint of heart! To be able to stand firm and against the messages of the culture that contradict our faith, we must dig our heels in and look to Jesus for strength and guidance. He gifts us with courage and grace to lead our children on the straight and narrow path that leads to heaven.

Family Prayer

All make the Sign of the Cross.

Parent: Dear Jesus, grant us courage to walk each day in faith.

Now let us listen to these words of Pope Francis.

A parent or child now reads the opening quotation aloud.

All: Blessed Mother Mary, bring us closer to your Son, Jesus.

A Story from Pope Francis's Life

Jorge worked as a chemical technician. Through prayer and reflection, he felt called to the priesthood, which was a vocation he had first heard when he was seventeen years old. It was on the Feast of Saint Matthew in 1953 when Jorge felt the call to religious life in the footsteps of Saint Ignatius of Loyola.

Before entering the seminary, Jorge was stricken at the age of twenty-one with a serious illness requiring hospitalization. He was diagnosed with severe pneumonia which eventually necessitated that part of his right lung be removed.

Fasting

Today, fast from fear. Any time you hesitate to follow God's teachings for fear of ridicule, actively ask for courage.

Almsgiving

Give ten minutes of your time to help bolster someone's faith.

Prayer

Today's Intention: Let's pray for those with a religious calling.

Closing Prayer: Dear Jesus, help our family to be courageous and loving helpers to others.

All pray the Our Father, Hail Mary, and Glory Be.

All through the Day: I want to remain steadfast on the journey of faith.

FRIDAY AFTER ASH WEDNESDAY

From the cross, Christ teaches us to love even those who do not love us.

—*Twitter, August 28, 2014*

Parent Reflection

So often we observe unjust things happening in the news or around us in our communities. We might have experienced bullying or persecution ourselves. We want to teach our children to love others, even those who treat us poorly. That doesn't mean that we go looking for abuse. But it does mean that as Christians we are called to love even when it is difficult. We are to forgive. Our example of Christian charity—real love and forgiveness—can be utterly transforming to those who receive it, who observe it in action, and even to ourselves. God has it all worked out. We need to respond lovingly to the opportunities that God allows.

Family Prayer

All make the Sign of the Cross.

> *Parent*: Dear Jesus, love through us. Allow us to be your love.

> Now let us listen to these words of Pope Francis.

A parent or child now reads the opening quotation aloud.

> *All*: Blessed Mother Mary, bring us closer to your Son, Jesus.

A Story from Pope Francis's Life

After a full recovery from the pneumonia and lung surgery, Jorge entered the Diocesan Seminary of Villo Devoto. He entered the novitiate of the Society of Jesus on March 11, 1958. Jorge took his first vows as a Jesuit on March 12, 1960. Jorge traveled to Padre Hurtado, Chile, to study, and there he completed his courses in the humanities.

In 1963, he returned to Argentina and graduated with a degree in philosophy from the Colegio de San José in San Miguel.

Fasting

Today, fast from judging others.

Almsgiving

Give away friendly and loving words to all you see today.

Prayer

> *Today's Intention:* Let's pray for those who do not show us love.

> *Closing Prayer:* Dear Jesus, help us to be a loving example to others.

> *All pray the Our Father, Hail Mary, and Glory Be.*

> *All through the Day:* I should count the many blessings God has given me.

Love shares everything it has and reveals itself in communication. There is no true faith that is not manifested in love. And love is not Christian love if it is not generous and concrete. A decidedly generous love is a sign of faith and an invitation to faith.

—*Lenten Letter, February 22, 2012*

Parent Reflection

Wow. According to Pope Francis, loving our children is a true sign of faith. And that act of loving also invites faith, he says. We are reminded that our love must be "generous and concrete" to be considered "Christian love." A loving Christian parent is familiar with generous loving because a good part of Christian parenting involves sacrifice. We must act with a generous heart to sacrifice for our children. We just need to ask our loving Father for help.

On this First Sunday of Lent, the gospel at Mass focuses on Jesus' temptation by the devil in the desert (Mt 4:1–11, Mk 1:12–15, Lk 4:1–13). The devil tried to persuade Jesus to think of his own needs, but Jesus would not turn away from his calling. It wasn't easy for Jesus and it can be difficult for us, too. But God will supply the graces we need.

Family Prayer

All make the Sign of the Cross.

> *Parent:* Dear Jesus, help our family to be open in communication and love with one another.

> Now let us listen to these words of Pope Francis.

A parent or child now reads the opening quotation aloud.

> *All:* Blessed Mother Mary, bring us closer to your Son, Jesus.

A Story from Pope Francis's Life

After years of study and graduating with degrees, Jorge began teaching high school literature and psychology at the Jesuit Immaculate Conception College in Santa Fe, Argentina. In 1966, he taught at the prestigious Colegio del Salvador in Buenos Aires. From 1967 to 1970, Jorge studied theology at San Miguel Seminary and obtained a degree from the Colegio de San José.

Fasting

Today, fast from spending time alone. Instead, get involved with the family.

Almsgiving

Think of a simple, loving way that your family can help others. Carry out the act this week.

Prayer

Today's Intention: Let's pray for those who don't have any immediate family.

Closing Prayer: Dear Jesus, help us to show our Christian love in concrete ways.

All pray the Our Father, Hail Mary, and Glory Be.

All through the Day: God wants me to love like him.

May we never get used to the poverty and decay around us.
A Christian must act.

—*Twitter, April 3, 2014*

Parent Reflection

One thing is for sure in our parenting: it is that we must always be ready to act—even when we are exhausted. We all know about those visits from our sick children in the middle of the night or our hungry babies calling to us, depending on us for nourishment at all hours, no matter how inconvenient it may seem. We jump into loving action. After all, it's what we do. We are situated in the hearts of our homes to act. There are also the times when we are called to act in our extended families, our neighborhoods, and our communities. We should take some time today to reflect on this fact: "A Christian must act." Perhaps you can brainstorm about how you can "act" as a family to help others throughout Lent.

Family Prayer

All make the Sign of the Cross.

> *Parent:* Dear Jesus, thank you for your love for us. Help us to love others with your love.

> Now let us listen to these words of Pope Francis.

A parent or child now reads the opening quotation aloud.

> *All:* Blessed Mother Mary, bring us closer to your Son, Jesus.

A Story from Pope Francis's Life

A few days before his thirty-third birthday, on December 13, 1969, Jorge was ordained a priest by Archbishop Ramón José Castellano. As a priest, Father Bergoglio continued his studies and training. Between 1970 and 1971, he studied at the University of Alcalá de Henares,

Spain. This was during his "tertianship," or the third period of Jesuit formation.

Fasting

Today, fast from a treat.

Almsgiving

Help a family member with a chore or task today without being asked.

Prayer

> *Today's Intention:* Let's pray for courage to allow God to act through us.
>
> *Closing Prayer:* Dear Jesus, help us to always look to you.
>
> *All pray the Our Father, Hail Mary, and Glory Be.*
>
> *All through the Day:* As a Christian, I must act always in accordance with God's will.

TUESDAY, FIRST WEEK OF LENT

We are not Christian "part time," only at certain moments, in certain circumstances, in certain decisions; no one can be Christian in this way—we are Christian all the time! Totally!
—*General Audience, May 15, 2013*

Parent Reflection

Pope Francis does not mince words. Neither does our Church. We are not to follow the teachings of the Church only when it is convenient. The teachings are life sustaining. Specifically, they are in place to guide us to heaven. Take some time today to ponder your behavior. Ask yourself if you are a Christian full time, at every moment—or not. At the dinner table tonight, talk to the children about this and encourage them to think about their own lives and how they can endeavor to be a full time Christian—"totally," as Pope Francis exclaimed.

Family Prayer

All make the Sign of the Cross.

Parent: Dear Jesus, guide our family each day throughout Lent to understand more fully what it means to be a Christian.

Now let us listen to these words of Pope Francis.

A parent or child now reads the opening quotation aloud.

All: Blessed Mother Mary, bring us closer to your Son, Jesus.

A Story from Pope Francis's Life

Not one to stand idle, between 1971 and 1973 Father Bergoglio served as novice master at Villa Barilari, San Miguel; professor on the Faculty of Theology of San Miguel; consulter to the Province of the Society of Jesus, and also the rector of the Colegio Máximo of the Faculty of

Philosophy and Theology. On April 22, 1973, at the age of thirty-six, Bergoglio made his final profession as a Jesuit.

Fasting

Today, fast from bickering. Tell the children if they wish to argue they should instead pause and say a prayer for that person.

Almsgiving

Give at least five minutes of prayer time for someone with whom you are at odds.

Prayer

> *Today's Intention*: Let's pray for our enemies and the enemies of the Church.
>
> *Closing Prayer*: Dear Jesus, help us to be full-time Christians—totally!
>
> *All pray the Our Father, Hail Mary, and Glory Be.*
>
> *All through the Day*: I will work at being a peacemaker.

WEDNESDAY, FIRST WEEK OF LENT

Do I pray? Do I speak with Jesus, or am I frightened of silence? Do I allow the Holy Spirit to speak to my heart? Do I ask Jesus: What do you want me to do, what do you want from my life? This is training. Ask Jesus, speak to Jesus, and if you make a mistake in your life, if you fall, if you should do something wrong, don't be afraid. [Say:] "Jesus, look at what I have done, what must I now do?"

—*Address, World Youth Day, July 27, 2013*

Parent Reflection

If it were not for prayer, what would we do? How could we even survive? Prayer is so necessary to be able to connect and converse with our loving God who gives us strength and grace to carry on. We must carve out time in our busy days to get to know God at a deeper level. If we don't schedule the time, the day might slip away in busyness or distraction. Take the time to retreat from the busyness, especially during this season of Lent. Seek the silence in which to converse with God and listen to what he is trying to whisper to your soul. This beautiful season is the perfect time to teach your children to take the time for prayer—not as a regimented requirement, but because we should *want* to talk with God. Let them know that Jesus loves them even when they make mistakes.

Family Prayer

All make the Sign of the Cross.

Parent: Dear Jesus, please remind us to listen to you.

Now let us listen to these words of Pope Francis.

A parent or child now reads the opening quotation aloud.

All: Blessed Mother Mary, bring us closer to your Son, Jesus.

A Story from Pope Francis's Life

Father Bergoglio was appointed the Provincial of the Jesuits in Argentina and Uruguay on July 31, 1973. He remained as a superior of the Jesuit Province for six years and continued his work in the university. After this, from 1980 to 1986, he served as a parish priest and again as a Rector of the Colegio de San José in San Miguel. After that, he would head to Germany.

Fasting

Today, fast from noise. It might be difficult, but try hard to find the quiet today. Or, make it happen.

Almsgiving

Give some time to God.

Prayer

Today's Intention: Let's pray for those who don't know how to pray.

Closing Prayer: Dear Jesus, help our family to always stay close to you.

All pray the Our Father, Hail Mary, and Glory Be.

All through the Day: I need to talk to and listen to Jesus!

Christ's love and his friendship are not an illusion—Jesus on the Cross shows how real they are—nor are they the privilege of a few.

You will discover this friendship and feel its fullness and beauty if you seek it with sincerity, open yourselves to him with trust, cultivate your spiritual life with perseverance, receiving the sacraments, meditating on Sacred Scripture, praying assiduously, and living with deep involvement in the Christian community.

—Message, June 21, 2013

Parent Reflection

We need one another. In the family and in the Body of Christ, we truly need each other. No man is an island. Because we are blessed to dwell within a family unit, we already have a community in which to grow in our faith. Pope Francis invites us to become deeply involved in the Christian community as well to cultivate our spiritual lives.

Parents have a unique role first and foremost as educators in the faith. This affords us a very direct, hands-on approach to our children's spiritual formation. Life in a family speaks volumes in itself. What can you do today and throughout the Lenten season to help your children grow in faith?

Family Prayer

All make the Sign of the Cross.

Parent: Dear Jesus, help us to realize our community of family within our domestic church and the need to be involved with the Christian community at large.

Now let us listen to these words of Pope Francis.

A parent or child now reads the opening quotation aloud.

All: Blessed Mother Mary, bring us closer to your Son, Jesus.

A Story from Pope Francis's Life

In 1985, Father Bergoglio became very inspired by the Marian example of Pope John Paul II (now a saint). He committed to praying all of the mysteries of the Rosary daily. In March 1986, Bergoglio was sent to Germany to finish his doctoral thesis. Afterward, his superiors decided to send him to the Colegio del Salvador in Buenos Aires. After some time there, he was sent to the Jesuit parish in the city of Córdoba, where he served as a confessor and spiritual director.

Fasting

Today, fast from teasing, ridicule, and being negative.

Almsgiving

Give a family member a surprise special message.

Prayer

Today's Intention: Let's pray for those who have wronged us in some way and for the persecuted.

Closing Prayer: Dear Jesus, help our family to be a light in the darkness of the world.

All pray the Our Father, Hail Mary, and Glory Be.

All through the Day: I am blessed to be a member of a family.

> Dear parents, teach your children to pray. Pray with them.
> —*Twitter, April 1, 2014*

Parent Reflection

Many times we are up against the clock and feel like we don't have enough time to complete our normal tasks. Because of our busyness, we can get pretty overwhelmed trying to find the time and the quiet in which to teach our children the invaluable lessons of cultivating a prayer life.

Yet if we start when the children are very young and naturally weave prayer into their lives, teaching them how to pray doesn't have to become a huge or impossible task. An important one—absolutely—but it can and should be accomplished each and every day. Your example of praying and your teaching will become etched on your children's hearts forever.

Family Prayer

All make the Sign of the Cross.

> *Parent:* Dear Jesus, please remind us about the important need to converse with you regularly.

Now let us listen to these words of Pope Francis.

A parent or child now reads the opening quotation aloud.

> *All:* Blessed Mother Mary, bring us closer to your Son, Jesus.

A Story from Pope Francis's Life

The Archbishop of Buenos Aires, Cardinal Antonio Quarracino, wanted Father Bergoglio as a close collaborator. So Pope John Paul II appointed him Titular Bishop of Auca and Auxiliary of Buenos Aires on May 20, 1992. He was ordained a bishop by the cardinal in the cathedral on May 27, 1992. As his Episcopal motto, Father Bergoglio chose *Miserando atque eligendo,* meaning "lowly but chosen": literally in Latin "by having mercy, by choosing him." He asked that the IHS, symbol of the Society of Jesus, be placed on his coat of arms.

Fasting

Today, fast from too much busyness as well as technology.

Almsgiving

Take ten to fifteen minutes to be quiet and pray.

Prayer

Today's Intention: Let's pray for those who have turned their backs on God.

Closing Prayer: Dear Jesus, help us to seek your guidance in all things.

All pray the Our Father, Hail Mary, and Glory Be.

All through the Day: Jesus loves me!

Let us remember well however, that whenever food is thrown out it is as if it were stolen from the table of the poor, from the hungry! I ask everyone to reflect on the problem of the loss and waste of food, to identify ways and approaches which, by seriously dealing with this problem, convey solidarity and sharing with the underprivileged.

—*General Audience, June 5, 2013*

Parent Reflection

Today is the Second Sunday of Lent. The gospels for the Church's three-year cycle of readings speak about the transfiguration of Jesus (Mt 17:1–9, Mk 9:2–10, Lk 9:28–36). Jesus revealed his glory to Peter, James, and John after taking them high up on a mountain. Jesus' face was shining as the sun and his clothes were a dazzling, pure white. A voice from a cloud said, "This is my beloved Son, with whom I am well pleased; listen to him" (Mt 17:5).

Filled with incredible fear, the disciples fell to the ground. Jesus reassured them and told them to get up. He explained that they should not tell anyone what they had witnessed until after he rose from the dead. The tremendous privilege of being shown Jesus this way and hearing God the Father speak gave Peter, James, and John much strength and nourishment for their journey ahead.

Pope Francis's words above speak about not wasting as well as our responsibility to care for the poor. Pope Francis reminds me of Mother Teresa whom I was very blessed to know personally. Both Mother Teresa and Pope Francis were very concerned about the poor and hungry. During the sacrificial season of Lent, what can your family do to help lessen the hunger pains of others? Will you fast this week and perhaps use the food you would have eaten and make something nutritious for the unfortunate in your community? Talk to the kids about ways you can help others as well as the importance of not wasting food.

Family Prayer

All make the Sign of the Cross.

> *Parent*: Dear Jesus, help us to never waste food that others could have eaten.

> Now let us listen to these words of Pope Francis.

A parent or child now reads the opening quotation aloud.

> *All*: Blessed Mother Mary, bring us closer to your Son, Jesus.

A Story from Pope Francis's Life

Bishop Bergoglio gave his very first interview as a bishop to *Estrellita de Belem*, a parish newsletter. Immediately after, on December 21, 1993, he was appointed the episcopal vicar of the Flores district. He was then entrusted with other responsibilities and appointed as the office of vicar general of the archdiocese.

Fasting

Today, fast from a treat.

Almsgiving

Today or sometime this week, make a meal for the needy and deliver it to a soup kitchen or family in need.

Prayer

> *Today's Intention*: Let's pray for the hungry all over the world.

> *Closing Prayer*: Dear Jesus, please take care of the hungry.

> *All pray the Our Father, Hail Mary, and Glory Be.*

> *All through the Day*: God is counting on me to do my part to serve the hungry.

In a family it is normal to take charge of those who need help. Do not be afraid of frailty!

—*Twitter, February 27, 2014*

Parent Reflection

The family unit can seem very frail at times and even completely broken. Its individual members can also be frail due to sickness and a variety of other reasons. Taking care of frailty can in many ways be daunting. Yet Pope Francis commands us not to be afraid.

What steps can you take during this season of pondering and praying to step up to the plate and throw away your fear?

Family Prayer

All make the Sign of the Cross.

Parent: Dear Jesus, give us courage.

Now let us listen to these words of Pope Francis.

A parent or child now reads the opening quotation aloud.

All: Blessed Mother Mary, bring us closer to your Son, Jesus.

A Story from Pope Francis's Life

Bishop Bergoglio seemed to be ascending the ranks, having been appointed to various new duties and positions including bishop, Episcopal Vicar, and Vicar General of the Archdiocese. He rose to each occasion. On June 3, 1997, he became the Coadjutor Archbishop of Buenos Aires.

Fasting

Today, fast from doubt.

Almsgiving

Throw away your fears and reach out in faith to aid someone.

Prayer

> *Today's Intention:* Let's pray for a deeper hope.
>
> *Closing Prayer:* Dear Jesus, I love you!
>
> *All pray the Our Father, Hail Mary, and Glory Be.*
>
> *All through the Day:* I'll stand steadfast in my faith.

TUESDAY, SECOND WEEK OF LENT

It is urgently necessary to find new forms and new ways to ensure that God's grace may touch the heart of every man and of every woman and lead them to him. We are all simple but important instruments of his; we have not received the gift of faith to keep it hidden, but, rather, to spread it so that it can illumine a great many of our brethren on their journey.

—*Address, May 17, 2013*

Parent Reflection

Our work is indeed cut out for us as Christian parents. We are hugely responsible for helping to shape the consciences of our children. Our Lord requires our wholehearted willingness to do all that is necessary to aid and teach them. Jesus also calls us to be a worthy example to everyone we come in contact with. We are a representative of the Church—whatever we do and say helps to transform lives. We cannot hide our Christian light under a bushel!

Family Prayer

All make the Sign of the Cross.

> *Parent*: Dear Jesus, please ignite a huge flame of faith in our hearts to share with others.

> Now let us listen to these words of Pope Francis.

A parent or child now reads the opening quotation aloud.

> *All*: Blessed Mother Mary, bring us closer to your Son, Jesus.

A Story from Pope Francis's Life

Not even nine months had passed after Bishop Bergoglio was appointed the coadjutor archbishop when, upon the death of Cardinal Quarracino, he was appointed as archbishop, primate of Argentina, and ordinary for Eastern-rite faithful in Argentina (who have no ordinary of their own rite) in February 1998.

Fasting

Today, fast from complacency (explain this to the kids). Act with faith instead.

Almsgiving

Give some time today to explaining some aspect of Christianity to someone.

Prayer

Today's Intention: Let's pray for our neighbors.

Closing Prayer: Dear Jesus, help us to spread your love.

All pray the Our Father, Hail Mary, and Glory Be.

All through the Day: God is counting on me to shine my light.

WEDNESDAY, SECOND WEEK OF LENT

The Cross is the word through which God has responded to evil in the world. Sometimes it may seem as though God does not react to evil, as if he is silent. And yet, God has spoken, he has replied, and his answer is the Cross of Christ; a word which is love, mercy, forgiveness.

—*Address, March 29, 2013*

Parent Reflection

This holy season of Lent is so much about the Cross of Christ. As you journey throughout this Lenten season, endeavor to teach your family more about the Cross of Christ. Encourage the family to take part in the Stations of the Cross on Fridays, which you can do together by going to your parish church and walking the Stations or by looking at images of the Stations in a book and praying them at home. Impress upon the children that they should be living their lives in imitation of Jesus' love, mercy, and forgiveness. Talk to them about this at the dinner table tonight and suggest ways they can do so.

Family Prayer

All make the Sign of the Cross.

Parent: Dear Jesus, help us to be more like you.

Now let us listen to these words of Pope Francis.

A parent or child now reads the opening quotation aloud.

All: Blessed Mother Mary, bring us closer to your Son, Jesus.

A Story from Pope Francis's Life

Pope John Paul II elevated Archbishop Bergoglio to a cardinal three years after he succeeded Cardinal Quarracino as primate of Argentina. The Holy Father assigned him the title of San Roberto Bellarmino. Bergoglio's love for the poor and his own humility were demonstrated when he asked the faithful not to come to Rome to celebrate his creation as cardinal. Instead, he suggested that they donate to the poor whatever the cost would have been to make the journey.

Fasting

Today, fast from fighting and arguing.

Almsgiving

Show mercy and forgiveness today.

Prayer

Today's Intention: Let's pray to be better Christians from now on.

Closing Prayer: Dear Jesus, we want to love and forgive like you.

All pray the Our Father, Hail Mary, and Glory Be.

All through the Day: Jesus is merciful and loving. I need to be as well.

THURSDAY, SECOND WEEK OF LENT

For us Christians, wherever the Cross is, there is hope, always. If there is no hope, we are not Christian. That is why I like to say: do not allow yourselves to be robbed of hope. May we not be robbed of hope, because this strength is a grace, a gift from God which carries us forward with our eyes fixed on heaven.

—*Homily, August 15, 2013*

Parent Reflection

Because life can sometimes seem so hard, we can lose hope if we are not careful. Pope Francis gives us the secret of retaining our hope. We must keep our eyes on heaven. We need to pray for the graces which are necessary to carry on. Christians should know that wherever the Cross is, there exists the miracle of abiding hope. Try your best to rely on the hope of the Cross even when everything looks dark or seems impossible. God is with you. Hang onto hope.

Family Prayer

All make the Sign of the Cross.

Parent: Dear Jesus, I need your graces and a huge dose of hope.

Now let us listen to these words of Pope Francis.

A parent or child now reads the opening quotation aloud.

All: Blessed Mother Mary, bring us closer to your Son, Jesus.

A Story from Pope Francis's Life

In Cardinal Bergoglio's position as grand chancellor of the Church University of Argentina, he authored three books: *Meditaciones para religiosos* (*Meditations for Religious*, 1982), *Reflexiones sobre la vida apostólica* (*Reflections on Apostolic Life*, 1992), and *Reflexiones de esperanza* (*Reflections of Hope*, 1992).

Fasting

Today, fast from any depressing or despairing thoughts. Keep your eyes on heaven.

Almsgiving

Give a gift of hope today. Help the children with ideas.

Prayer

> *Today's Intention:* Let's pray for those in areas in the world where hope seems lost.
>
> *Closing Prayer:* Dear Jesus, help us to be a ray of hope to others.
>
> *All pray the Our Father, Hail Mary, and Glory Be.*
>
> *All through the Day:* I need to keep my eyes on heaven and ask God for grace.

FRIDAY, SECOND WEEK OF LENT

Speak continually with Jesus, in the good times and in the bad, when you do right and when you do wrong. Do not fear him! This is prayer.

—*Address, World Youth Day, July 27, 2013*

Parent Reflection

Get in the habit of offering your day to the Lord first thing every morning. Offer all of your prayers, works, joys, and sufferings in the words of the formal Morning Offering or in your own words. Ask God to take care of everything. After getting your day off to the right start, try to lift up your heart to Jesus all throughout the day. Tell the children to do the same. As Pope Francis says, "This is prayer."

By forming the habit of taking the time in the morning and throughout the day, you'll be keeping up a conversation with Jesus. In addition, your family time of prayer together in following this Lenten guide will deepen this conversation. It will be a practice long remembered by your children and hopefully carried on in the future in their own domestic churches.

Family Prayer

All make the Sign of the Cross.

Parent: Dear Jesus, keep us in a loving conversation with you.

Now let us listen to these words of Pope Francis.

A parent or child now reads the opening quotation aloud.

All: Blessed Mother Mary, bring us closer to your Son, Jesus.

A Story from Pope Francis's Life

Cardinal Bergoglio was appointed general relator to the Tenth Ordinary General Assembly of the Synod of Bishops on the Episcopal Ministry in October 2001. He was entrusted with this task to replace

Cardinal Edward Michael Egan, archbishop of New York, who was suddenly obliged to stay in his homeland because of the attacks of September 11, 2001.

Fasting

Today, fast from technology as best as you can.

Almsgiving

Give Jesus a half hour of quiet time today to listen to him speak to your heart.

Prayer

Today's Intention: Let's pray for peace in the world.

Closing Prayer: Dear Jesus, help us to realize the importance of prayer.

All pray the Our Father, Hail Mary, and Glory Be.

All through the Day: I will give my heart to Jesus.

THIRD SUNDAY OF LENT

We cannot become starched Christians, those over-educated Christians who speak of theological matters as they calmly sip their tea. No! We must become courageous Christians and go in search of the people who are the very flesh of Christ!

—Address, *Vigil of Pentecost with Ecclesial Movements, May 18, 2013*

Parent Reflection

Today is the Third Sunday of Lent. Although different, all of the gospels for the Church's three-year cycle of readings invite us to remember the words of Ash Wednesday: "Turn away from sin and be faithful to the Gospel." They invite us to a conversion of heart.

Jesus invited the Samaritan woman to repent of her sins and drink the Living Water (Jn 4:5–42) to be truly converted. Jesus cleansed the temple (Jn 2:13–25) and forcefully ejected the moneychangers. Finally, Jesus gave the example of the barren fig tree (Lk 13:1–9) to remind us of God's great patience with us even in our failures.

Our Church reminds us in so many ways of our duty to serve one another. Pope Francis's words above tell us to become courageous and go out and search for the "very flesh of Christ." Mother Teresa spoke much about the need to serve Jesus in one another. She wholeheartedly believed that Jesus lives in those we serve and that Jesus also calls us to serve him, especially when he said, "Truly I tell you, just as you did it to one of the least of these who are members of the family, you did it to me" (Mt 25:40). Start reaching out within your own family and when all are satisfied, broaden your reach.

Family Prayer

All make the Sign of the Cross.

> *Parent:* Dear Jesus, help us to always recognize you in others.

Now let us listen to these words of Pope Francis.

A parent or child now reads the opening quotation aloud.

All: Blessed Mother Mary, bring us closer to your Son, Jesus.

A Story from Pope Francis's Life

After suddenly acquiring the role of general relator to the Synod of Bishops on the Episcopal Ministry, Cardinal Bergoglio placed particular emphasis on the prophetic mission of the bishop, his being a prophet of justice, his particular duty to preach ceaselessly the social teaching of the Church, and also to express an authentic judgment in matters of faith and morals.

Fasting

Today, fast from a comfort. Taking a shorter shower, getting up from bed earlier, or eating less are some examples.

Almsgiving

Give time away today. Help a family member with a chore.

Prayer

Today's Intention: Let's pray for those who suffer in silence.

Closing Prayer: Dear Jesus, help us to recognize the needs of our family members and those who are near.

All pray the Our Father, Hail Mary, and Glory Be.

All through the Day: There's a time to sip tea and a time to act.

Remain steadfast in the journey of faith, with firm hope in the Lord. This is the secret of our journey! He gives us courage to swim against the tide. Pay attention . . . go against the current; this is good for the heart, but we need courage to swim against the tide. Jesus gives us this courage!

—*Homily, Holy Mass of Confirmation, April 28, 2013*

Parent Reflection

Raising children in today's fast-paced world is not for the timid, especially when striving to teach our children the right way—God's way. It would be so much easier to give in and to go with the flow of the world. But we must keep in mind that to do so would be like escorting our children and ourselves, for that matter, to hell! Strong words, yes, but true.

Family Prayer

All make the Sign of the Cross.

> *Parent:* Dear Jesus, give us the courage to turn away from the allurements of the world.

Now let us listen to these words of Pope Francis.

A parent or child now reads the opening quotation aloud.

> *All:* Blessed Mother Mary, bring us closer to your Son, Jesus.

A Story from Pope Francis's Life

Cardinal Bergoglio lived a strict lifestyle which some have referred to as "ascetic." He lived a spirit of poverty and was very beloved by the people of Latin America. Retaining that spirit, all throughout his Episcopal ministry Cardinal Bergoglio traveled by bus or subway rather than a more affluent mode of transportation. Because of his commitment to a simple ascetic lifestyle, he declined to be appointed as President of the Argentine Bishops' Conference in 2002.

Fasting

Today, fast from television.

Almsgiving

Encourage the children to write a hopeful poem or a letter to someone in need.

Prayer

Today's Intention: Let's pray for all those who feel hopeless.

Closing Prayer: Dear Jesus, help us to spread your love and truth.

All pray the Our Father, Hail Mary, and Glory Be.

All through the Day: God is counting on me to be a good Christian example.

TUESDAY, THIRD WEEK OF LENT

To live by faith means to put our lives in the hands of God, especially in our most difficult moments.

—*Twitter, May 23, 2014*

Parent Reflection

I don't think there is one parent alive who doesn't understand what it means to deal with difficult moments in parenting their children. Even the Blessed Mother experienced difficult moments. In fact, she experienced many. Parents face uncertainty on any given day. Pope Francis encourages us to "put our lives in the hands of God, especially in our most difficult moments" if we are to live by faith. Doing so is truly the best means to living out our vocation authentically and will reap the benefit of much grace.

Family Prayer

All make the Sign of the Cross.

> *Parent*: Dear Jesus, help us to trust you more.

> Now let us listen to these words of Pope Francis.

A parent or child now reads the opening quotation aloud.

> *All*: Blessed Mother Mary, bring us closer to your Son, Jesus.

A Story from Pope Francis's Life

Though Cardinal Bergoglio initially declined the appointment as president of the Argentine Bishops' Conference, three years later he was elected. In 2008, he was reconfirmed for an additional three-year mandate. During that time, in April, 2005, Cardinal Bergoglio took part in the conclave at which Pope Benedict XVI was elected.

Fasting

Today, fast from a treat.

Almsgiving

Take the time to truly thank Jesus for your family and endeavor to reach out in love to a family member most in need of that love.

Prayer

Today's Intention: Let's pray for peace in the world.

Closing Prayer: Dear Jesus, thank you for your great love for our family.

All pray the Our Father, Hail Mary, and Glory Be.

All through the Day: I am to be a vessel of God's love to others.

How beautiful it is to stand before the Crucifix, simply to be under the Lord's gaze, so full of love.

—*Twitter, April 12, 2014*

Parent Reflection

When we gaze upon a crucifix we generally first imagine the injustice and also the pain inflicted upon Christ. Pope Francis suggests that we find love in Our Lord's gaze. Take time today to ponder Jesus' crucifixion and death, but also his resurrection and ascension to heaven. Talk to the kids about the meaning of Jesus' death on the Cross.

Family Prayer

All make the Sign of the Cross.

> *Parent*: Dear Jesus, thank you for dying on the cross for me. Thank you for loving me that much!

> Now let us listen to these words of Pope Francis.

A parent or child now reads the opening quotation aloud.

> *All*: Blessed Mother Mary, bring us closer to your Son, Jesus.

A Story from Pope Francis's Life

Archbishop Bergoglio was full of good and holy ideas and goals. As Archbishop of Buenos Aires, a city comprised of more than three million inhabitants, he developed a missionary project based on communion and evangelization. He wanted to re-evangelize Buenos Aires. His four major goals were for open and brotherly communities, an informed laity playing a lead role, evangelization efforts addressed to every inhabitant of the city, and assistance to the poor and the sick.

Fasting

Today, fast from selfishness and spending time on comforts.

Almsgiving

Gaze upon a crucifix today and pray to understand the meaning of Jesus' crucifixion.

Prayer

Today's Intention: Let's pray for the poorest of the poor all over the world.

Closing Prayer: Dear Jesus, help me to think more of others rather than myself.

All pray the Our Father, Hail Mary, and Glory Be.

All through the Day: God wants me to be generous with others.

THURSDAY, THIRD WEEK OF LENT

It is not easy to follow Jesus closely, because the path he chooses is the way of the Cross.

—*Twitter, April 18, 2014*

Parent Reflection

It might not seem natural to desire to choose the way of the Cross. Yet, that is the path that Jesus chose and the very path he tells us to follow. As difficult as it might seem, we can truly learn to love following the right path. We will when our heart is in the right place. Take time today to reflect on Jesus' life. Read this Scripture verse at the dinner table.

> If any want to become my followers, let them deny themselves and take up their cross and follow me. For those who want to save their life will lose it, and those who lose their life for my sake will find it. For what will it profit them if they gain the whole world but forfeit their life? Or what will they give in return for their life? (Matthew 16:24–26)

Family Prayer

All make the Sign of the Cross.

Parent: Dear Jesus, help our family to come closer to you.

Now let us listen to these words of Pope Francis.

A parent or child now reads the opening quotation aloud.

All: Blessed Mother Mary, bring us closer to your Son, Jesus.

A Story from Pope Francis's Life

As part of his efforts to re-evangelize Buenos Aires, Cardinal Bergoglio asked priests and the laity to work together. He said his efforts to re-evangelize would be "taking into account those who live here, its structure and its history." He launched the solidarity campaign for the bicentenary of the independence of the country in September 2009.

Fasting

Today, fast from noise and activity as much as possible.

Almsgiving

Make a phone call, or write an e-mail or a letter, to someone who needs encouragement.

Prayer

Today's Intention: Let's pray for the sick and unfortunate.

Closing Prayer: Dear Jesus, help us to follow you.

All pray the Our Father, Hail Mary, and Glory Be.

All through the Day: Following Jesus will lead me to heaven.

Let each one ask him- or herself today: "Do I increase harmony in my family, in my parish, in my community, or am I a gossip? Am I a cause of division or embarrassment?" And you know the harm that gossiping does to the Church, to the parishes, the communities. Gossip does harm! Gossip wounds.

Before Christians open their mouths to gossip, they should bite their tongues! To bite one's tongue: this does us good because the tongue swells and can no longer speak, cannot gossip. "Am I humble enough to patiently stitch up, through sacrifice, the open wounds in communion?"

—*General Audience, September 25, 2013*

Parent Reflection

Temptations to gossip abound for both adults and children alike. As adults though, we should know better. We should never gossip. Take some time today to discuss the problems and pain that Pope Francis talks about. Tell the children that to be humble and rise above the temptation to gossip makes them a better and wiser person. They can be a stellar example to their peers and please God.

Family Prayer

All make the Sign of the Cross.

Parent: Dear Jesus, help us to be humble and loving.

Now let us listen to these words of Pope Francis.

A parent or child now reads the opening quotation aloud.

All: Blessed Mother Mary, bring us closer to your Son, Jesus.

A Story from Pope Francis's Life

In setting up the solidarity campaign for the bicentenary of the independence of Argentina in 2010, Cardinal Bergoglio set a goal to create two hundred charitable agencies by 2016. He described the Aparecida Conference in 2007 as the "Evangelization in the Modern World" (the apostolic exhortation of Pope Paul VI) of Latin America and expected much from its impact. He described the concluding document of the conference the result of "working from the bottom up, not the opposite."

Fasting

Today, fast from gossiping and any temptation to be prideful.

Almsgiving

Make a point to place emphasis on others' good words and accomplishments.

Prayer

Today's Intention: Let's pray for those who are arrogant and who have been condescending toward us.

Closing Prayer: Dear Jesus, help us to light the way for others with your love.

All pray the Our Father, Hail Mary, and Glory Be.

All through the Day: I should never gossip or hurt another with my words.

FOURTH SUNDAY OF LENT

The weight of our cross frees us from all of our burdens. In our obedience to the Father's will, we notice our rebellion and disobedience. . . . Let the feelings of faith, hope, charity, and sorrow for our sins be ingrained in our hearts, Lord, and lead us to repent for our sins that have crucified you. . . . Crucified Jesus, strengthen the faith in us so that it not give in before temptations, rekindle hope in us so that it not get lost by following the world's seductions. Protect charity in us so that it not be deceived by corruption and worldliness. Teach us that the cross is the way to resurrection.

— *Reflections after the Way of the Cross, April 3, 2015*

Parent Reflection

Today is the Fourth Sunday of Lent. All three gospel readings for the three cycles of Lent offer perspectives on Jesus, the Light of the World: the man born blind (Cycle A), Jesus meeting Nicodemus at night (Cycle B), and the prodigal son (Cycle C).

The story of the man born blind (Jn 9:1–41) speaks to us about faith. The faithful man receives physical and spiritual sight while those around him seem "blind" and lacking in faith. The prodigal son parable (Lk 15:1–3, 11–32) illustrates a wayward son who sees the "light"—the error of his ways— and repents and begs his father's mercy. His brother is "blind" to his own selfishness and his father's mercy. In the next story, Nicodemus (Jn 3:14–21) sought out Jesus in the night because he was fearful to be seen with Jesus. Nonetheless, he was drawn to the light of Christ. Jesus explained to Nicodemus, "But whoever lives in truth comes to the light, so that his works may be clearly seen as done in God."

Pope Francis speaks about Christ's Cross in his words above. In meditating on the Cross of Christ, we might consider that something that appears to be so ugly, cruel, and evil has in reality brought about miraculous love, mercy, and forgiveness. Such is the mystery of the Cross of Christ in God's great love for us. During this season of Lent, ponder ways that you can offer up any of your difficulties, inconveniences, or sufferings to Jesus and ask him to sanctify them and transform them into graces for your family members. Teach the kids to not waste their sufferings. Ask them to "offer it up" to God when they don't feel well or are upset. God will grant them graces for lovingly doing so.

Family Prayer

All make the Sign of the Cross.

Parent: Dear Jesus, I want to learn to be more patient when I am uncomfortable or suffering in some way.

Now let us listen to these words of Pope Francis.

A parent or child now reads the opening quotation aloud.

All: Blessed Mother Mary, bring us closer to your Son, Jesus.

A Story from Pope Francis's Life

Cardinal Bergoglio was a very busy man of God. He was a member of the Congregation for Divine Worship and the Discipline of the Sacraments, the Congregation for the Clergy, the Congregation for Institutes of Consecrated Life and Societies of Apostolic Life, the Pontifical Council for the Family, and the Pontifical Commission for Latin America.

Fasting

Today, fast from complaining or grumbling.

Almsgiving

Offer a sacrifice to God today. It can be very simple but done with love. Offer it to God for a family member's benefit.

Prayer

Today's Intention: Let's pray for those who do not believe in God.

Closing Prayer: Dear Jesus, I'm sorry for all of my complaining. I love you and I love my life.

All pray the Our Father, Hail Mary, and Glory Be.

All through the Day: God wants me to show his love.

MONDAY, FOURTH WEEK OF LENT

To live charitably means not looking out for our own interests but carrying the burdens of the weakest and poorest among us.

—*Twitter, November 25, 2013*

Parent Reflection

Certainly the "weakest and poorest" among us are our children. Parents indeed carry the burdens of their children all throughout raising them. There's the pain we feel in our own hearts when our children have been hurt or have endured sickness or anguish. There is the thorn of inadequacy we sometimes feel inside when we cannot fix everything in our children's lives. But God doesn't expect us to fix everything. He wants us to do the best we can in raising our children—yes, to carry their burdens in a sense, but first and foremost, to trust all of the burdens to him. Ponder that today.

Family Prayer

All make the Sign of the Cross.

> *Parent:* Dear Jesus, help our family to open our hearts to the needs around us.

> Now let us listen to these words of Pope Francis.

A parent or child now reads the opening quotation aloud.

> *All:* Blessed Mother Mary, bring us closer to your Son, Jesus.

A Story from Pope Francis's Life

On March 13, 2013, Jorge Mario Bergoglio, seventy-six-year-old Jesuit, cardinal, and archbishop of Buenos Aires, was elected supreme pontiff. He is the first pope of the Americas. He was a prominent figure throughout the continent and is still beloved by his diocese. The people from his homeland were ecstatic over his election as pope. That very day, the new pontiff visited the Basilica of St. Mary Major in Rome to entrust his papacy to the Blessed Mother.

Fasting

Today, fast from worrying. Take steps to trust God instead.

Almsgiving

Give a gift of love to a family member (a handmade card, a note, a surprise act of kindness).

Prayer

Today's Intention: Let's pray for all of the lonely and forgotten.

Closing Prayer: Dear Jesus, help us to spread your love to all we meet, beginning in our family.

All pray the Our Father, Hail Mary, and Glory Be.

All through the Day: God gives us strength to carry other's burdens.

Pursuing and accumulating power as some form of adrenaline . . . leads to self-destruction. . . . Real power is love; love that empowers others, love that sparks initiatives, love that no chain can hold because this love is capable of loving even on the cross or on a deathbed. It has no need of youthful beauty, recognition or approval, money or prestige. It simply flows forth and is unstoppable. When slandered or defeated, it unquestionably acquires greater recognition.

The Jesus who was weak and insignificant in the eyes of politicians and the powerful of the land revolutionized the world.

—*Homily, May 25, 2012*

Parent Reflection

R eal love is truly unstoppable. Can you think of a time in your life when love took over and it didn't matter how bogged down you were or how bad the situation? Love took over. And, God came through. God always comes through but sometimes it is much more obvious to us than at other times. Take some time today, even fifteen minutes, to reflect on Jesus' unstoppable, powerful love for you from the Cross.

Family Prayer

All make the Sign of the Cross.

Parent: Dear Jesus, your love revolutionized the world. Please bring your love into our hearts.

Now let us listen to these words of Pope Francis.

A parent or child now reads the opening quotation aloud.

All: Blessed Mother Mary, bring us closer to your Son, Jesus.

A Story from Pope Francis's Life

Pope Francis made it very clear that he wanted to retain a spirit of poverty even though he was the pope. Soon after assuming his new role, he said, "My people are poor and I am one of them." He chose to live in an apartment and cook his own meals rather than live in the papal apartments in the Apostolic Palace where people would wait on him.

Fasting

Today, fast from talking too much. Look for quiet today.

Almsgiving

Give time to God in silence today. Ponder Jesus dying on the Cross for you.

Prayer

> *Today's Intention:* Let's pray for all those unjustly accused.
>
> *Closing Prayer:* Dear Jesus, strengthen our family in love.
>
> *All pray the Our Father, Hail Mary, and Glory Be.*
>
> *All through the Day:* Christ's love can revolutionize the world!

Trust in the power of Christ's Cross! Receive his reconciling grace and share it!

—*Twitter, August 18, 2014*

Parent Reflection

Holy Mother Church constantly guides us on our journey to heaven. She offers the sacraments because Jesus himself gave them to the Church. The Sacrament of Confession frees us and gives us so much grace. There's no need to fear the Sacrament. Take time today to talk with the kids about forgiveness, reconciliation, and the wonderful benefits of the Sacrament of Confession. Ask them to forgive one another in the family as well as others outside the family. Ask them to recall a time when someone has hurt them in some way and encourage them to forgive them wholeheartedly. Have you scheduled a time to bring the family to confession? Get to confession as a family soon and continue the teaching of God's reconciling grace to the kids.

Family Prayer

All make the Sign of the Cross.

> *Parent*: Dear Jesus, grant me your reconciling graces and help me to forgive others.

> Now let us listen to these words of Pope Francis.

A parent or child now reads the opening quotation aloud.

> *All*: Blessed Mother Mary, bring us closer to your Son, Jesus.

A Story from Pope Francis's Life

In his encyclical letter *The Light of Faith*, Pope Francis speaks about God's love. He said, "Faith is born of an encounter with the living God who calls us and reveals his love, a love which precedes us and upon which we can lean for security and for building our lives. Transformed by this love, we gain fresh vision, new eyes to see; we realize that it contains a great promise of fulfillment, and that a vision of the future opens up before us" (no. 4).

Fasting

Today, fast from judging. If the temptation arises, say a prayer.

Almsgiving

Help the children write a note of reconciliation to a family member or friend.

Prayer

>*Today's Intention:* Let's pray for all who have hurt us in some way.

>*Closing Prayer:* Dear Jesus, help me to always trust in the power of your Cross.

>*All pray the Our Father, Hail Mary, and Glory Be.*

>*All through the Day:* Jesus' love is powerful!

The cross is the price of true love. Lord, give us the strength to accept and carry our crosses!

—Twitter, December 6, 2013

Parent Reflection

Life in the family is full of excitement. There never seems to be a dull moment. But some of those moments are painful or challenging. This can be due to sickness, financial stress, or any number of other tough issues. Our Lord asks us to carry our crosses with love and acceptance. Pope Francis encourages us to ask God for strength to do so. Take some time today to explain to the family that especially during this season, which is meant to be penitential, we should work at carrying our crosses without grumbling and complaining. Yes, we ask God to relieve us of the crosses if it is his holy will. Otherwise, we trust that God knows what is best.

Family Prayer

All make the Sign of the Cross.

Parent: Dear Jesus, help us to offer our hearts to you with love.

Now let us listen to these words of Pope Francis.

A parent or child now reads the opening quotation aloud.

All: Blessed Mother Mary, bring us closer to your Son, Jesus.

A Story from Pope Francis's Life

In *The Light of Faith,* Pope Francis encourages those who might feel isolated, lost, or in the dark when he says, "Faith, received from God as a supernatural gift, becomes a light for our way, guiding our journey through time. On the one hand, it is a light coming from the past, the light of the foundational memory of the life of Jesus which revealed his perfectly trustworthy love, a love capable of triumphing over death. Yet since Christ has risen and draws us beyond death, faith is also a light coming from the future and opening before us vast horizons which guide us beyond our isolated selves toward the breadth of communion. We come to see that faith does not dwell in shadow and gloom; it is a light for our darkness."

Fasting

Today, fast from a treat.

Almsgiving

Give extra time in prayer today.

Prayer

Today's Intention: Let's pray for those who are suffering because of war or terrorism of some kind.

Closing Prayer: Dear Jesus, help me to see you in others.

All pray the Our Father, Hail Mary, and Glory Be.

All through the Day: Jesus died for me.

The Lord always forgives us and walks at our side. We have to let him do that.

—*Twitter, August 30, 2013*

Parent Reflection

This is another good day to teach the kids about forgiveness and love. Pray the Our Father slowly when you pray together. Point out to the children the line, "Forgive us our trespasses as we forgive those who trespass against us." Ask what it means to them. Allow them to ponder and share. Remind them that they are to forgive others if they expect God to forgive them.

Family Prayer

All make the Sign of the Cross.

> *Parent*: Dear Jesus, grant us the grace to love our enemy and those who have hurt us.

> Now let us listen to these words of Pope Francis.

A parent or child now reads the opening quotation aloud.

> *All*: Blessed Mother Mary, bring us closer to your Son, Jesus.

A Story from Pope Francis's Life

In his encyclical letter *The Light of Faith*, Pope Francis stressed the need for the light of faith, especially in our world today. He said, "Dante, in the *Divine Comedy*, after professing his faith to Saint Peter, describes that light as a 'spark, which then becomes a burning flame and like a heavenly star within me glimmers.' It is this light of faith that I would now like to consider, so that it can grow and enlighten the present, becoming a star to brighten the horizon of our journey at a time when mankind is particularly in need of light."

Fasting

Today, fast from any arguing. When tempted to "be right," say a quiet prayer instead of trying to prove yourself.

Almsgiving

Let today's "alms" be a surprise to a family member. Encourage the kids to come up with ideas.

Prayer

Today's Intention: Let's pray for the souls in purgatory.

Closing Prayer: Dear Jesus, help us to forgive others with a cheerful heart.

All pray the Our Father, Hail Mary, and Glory Be.

All through the Day: God wants me to reach out with his love.

FIFTH SUNDAY OF LENT

Miracles happen but prayer is needed! Prayer that is courageous, struggling, and persevering, not prayer that is a mere
formality.

—*Twitter, May 24, 2013*

Parent Reflection

Today is the Fifth Sunday in Lent. In the three gospels, we hear
about the raising of Lazarus (Jn 11:1–45), Jesus speaks of his coming death (Jn 12:20–33), and the story of the woman caught in adultery
(Jn 8:1–11). Jesus teaches us that we all must rise from our sin to new
life. He says, "Amen, amen, I say to you, unless a grain of wheat falls
to the ground and dies, it remains just a grain of wheat; but if it dies,
it produces much fruit"(Jn 12:24).The raising of Lazarus was a sign
of this. He was not resurrected as Jesus was, but nonetheless, he was
resuscitated. It points to Jesus' rising and the power of Christ to raise
us up out of our sin to new life. The woman caught in adultery was
also raised to a new life. Jesus' love and immense mercy saved her
physically and, more important, forgave her and gave her new life.

In Pope Francis's words above, he stresses the miraculous power
in prayer. Parents pray many sorts of prayers. At times, the prayers
are expressed from our hearts with ease. At other times, we struggle to
speak to God from our hearts when we or our children are suffering
in some way. Yet we know that we need to persevere in our prayers to
a loving God who knows what is best for our hearts and souls. Jesus
never said that this life will be easy. In fact, our Lord told us that we
need to pick up our crosses and follow him. Let's be sure our prayers
do not become a mere formality. Let's endeavor to get to know our
Lord more intimately so we can more freely share our hearts with him.
God will grant us the graces to walk in faith courageously each day.

Family Prayer

All make the Sign of the Cross.

Parent: Dear Jesus, forgive us for our laziness in prayer. Help us to put our hearts into our conversations with you.

Now let us listen to these words of Pope Francis.

A parent or child now reads the opening quotation aloud.

All: Blessed Mother Mary, bring us closer to your Son, Jesus.

A Story from Pope Francis's Life

In 1986, before Pope Francis was a pope, he visited Germany and was captivated upon seeing a painting of the Blessed Mother untying knots in a white ribbon. The story dates back to 1612 when a German couple who had marital trouble were on the verge of divorce. A Jesuit priest held up their wedding ribbon before an image of Mary and prayed that "all knots be loosened and resolved." The unknotted ribbon became bright white and their marriage survived. Mary had interceded. Pope Francis is attributed to having written his own prayer in devotion to Our Lady, Undoer of Knots.

Fasting

Today, fast from rushing through prayers and spiritual studies.

Almsgiving

Give time to our Lord today. You decide what that will consist of.

Prayer

Today's Intention: Let's pray for those who do not know God.

Closing Prayer: Dear Jesus, forgive my apathy at times. I want my heart to grow more in love with you each day!

All pray the Our Father, Hail Mary, and Glory Be.

All through the Day: I love you, Jesus, my love.

At times we can be self-absorbed. Lord, help us to open our hearts to others and to serve those who are most vulnerable.
—*Twitter, June 2, 2014*

Parent Reflection

There can be no doubt that God made babies so darn cute and vulnerable because it draws our hearts to want to love them and care for them. When they belt out screeches in the night, waking us from a sound sleep, we remember their vulnerability and refrain from feeling annoyed because we were suddenly roused from our slumber. This is not the time to be self-absorbed. Babies and children need us, after all. We open our hearts and our lives fully to our children.

At times in life, we can become self-absorbed if we are not careful. In the course of the day, as we are involved with our devices (phones, tablets, computers, and our work or pleasures), we can miss observing the needs of those who are around us at home, in the neighborhood, or the workplace. But, we can daily choose to become more cognizant of those who need our attention and love. Let's lift our eyes from our technological devices to see what's going on around us!

Family Prayer

All make the Sign of the Cross.

> *Parent*: Dear Jesus, help me open my eyes and my heart to those in my life who need me to help them.

Now let us listen to these words of Pope Francis.

A parent or child now reads the opening quotation aloud.

> *All*: Blessed Mother Mary, bring us closer to your Son, Jesus.

A Story from Pope Francis's Life

Not one to ever forget about the needy and with a heart full of love for the poor, sick, and unfortunate, Pope Francis includes loving directives to the faithful in his apostolic exhortation *The Joy of the Gospel* when he says, "When we read the Gospel we find a clear indication: not so much our friends and wealthy neighbours, but above all the poor and the sick, those who are usually despised and overlooked, 'those who cannot repay you' (Lk 14:14)" (par. 48).

Fasting

Today, fast from being self-absorbed.

Almsgiving

Give a special gift of care today to someone at home. Help the kids with this.

Prayer

Today's Intention: Let's pray for those who feel unloved or forgotten.

Closing Prayer: Dear Jesus, help me to be your instrument of love and care.

All pray the Our Father, Hail Mary, and Glory Be.

All through the Day: Jesus wants me to give away his love to others.

Mary saw many difficult moments in her life, from the birth of Jesus, when "there was no place for them in the inn" (Lk 2:7), to Calvary (cf. Jn 19:25). And like a good mother, she is close to us, so that we never lose courage before the adversities of life, before our weakness, before our sins: she gives us strength, she shows us the path of her Son.

—*Address, May 4, 2013*

Parent Reflection

Do you have images of the Blessed Mother in your home, your little domestic church? I came to know Mother Mary because my grandmother and mother displayed sacred images throughout their homes. They drew my heart to Mother Mary who leads me to her Son, Jesus. My mother called her children together as often as possible to pray the Rosary. It was more like rustling cattle, to tell you the truth, getting all eight of us kids together at the same time. But she did succeed, and I am grateful that she did introduce me to Mother Mary. Throughout the Lenten season, endeavor to teach your children more about the Blessed Mother. Talk about her at the dinner table tonight.

Family Prayer

All make the Sign of the Cross.

> *Parent:* Dear Jesus, thank you for the gift of your Mother.

> Now let us listen to these words of Pope Francis.

A parent or child now reads the opening quotation aloud.

> *All:* Blessed Mother Mary, bring us closer to your Son, Jesus.

A Story from Pope Francis's Life

Pope Francis won't let us forget about the beloved poor and tells us, in his apostolic exhortation *The Joy of the Gospel*, "I can say that the most beautiful and natural expressions of joy which I have seen in my life were in poor people who had little to hold on to" (par. 07).

Fasting

Today, fast from television and the Internet as much as possible.

Almsgiving

Give some time to Mother Mary today in prayer and in learning more about her through spiritual reading.

Prayer

> *Today's Intention:* Let's pray for children all around the world to grow to be amazing Christians.
>
> *Closing Prayer:* Dear Jesus, help our family to spread your love.
>
> *All pray the Our Father, Hail Mary, and Glory Be.*
>
> *All through the Day:* Mother Mary understands our joys and troubles and brings us closer to her Son.

WEDNESDAY, FIFTH WEEK OF LENT

Time is the messenger of God: God saves us in time, not in a moment. At times he works miracles, but in everyday life he saves us through time.

Sometimes we think that if the Lord comes into our life, he will change us. Yes, we do change: it is called conversion. But he does not act like "a fairy with a magic wand." No. He gives you the grace and he says, as he said to everyone he healed: "Go, walk."

—*Homily, Domus Sanctae Marthae, April 12, 2013*

Parent Reflection

Life in the family is filled with unexpected blessings. Some are in the form of experiences that we might prefer not to have. Others are comprised of profound joy. With God's grace, they can all be amazing opportunities for conversion and spiritual growth. Conversion is not a once-in-a-lifetime experience. It happens every day. We need to "go, walk" closer and closer to heaven each day by putting one foot in front of the other in faith, not expecting a magic wand to get us there.

Family Prayer

All make the Sign of the Cross.

Parent: Dear Jesus, help us to walk in faith each day closer to you.

Now let us listen to these words of Pope Francis.

A parent or child now reads the opening quotation aloud.

All: Blessed Mother Mary, bring us closer to your Son, Jesus.

A Story from Pope Francis's Life

On October 13, 2013, after a weekend of Marian prayer, tens of thousands of pilgrims from all over the world gathered in St. Peter's Square to witness Pope Francis consecrating the world to the Immaculate

Heart of Mary. It was the ninety-sixth anniversary of the Blessed Mother's appearance to Jacinta and Francesco Marto and Lucia dos Santos at Fatima. The original statue of Our Lady of Fatima had been transferred from the Shrine of Our Lady of Fatima in Portugal to St. Peter's Square for the occasion.

During his address on the momentous occasion, Pope Francis emphasized that the Virgin Mary leads all to the mercy of God, who can untie "all knotted hearts" caused by sin. "These knots take away our peace and serenity," he said.

Pope Francis asked the Blessed Mother to accept and welcome the consecration "with the benevolence of a mother."

Fasting

Today, fast from doubt, negativity, and even complacency. Explain this to the kids.

Almsgiving

Give some time in spiritual reading. If possible, read about a saint at the dinner table.

Prayer

> *Today's Intention:* Let's pray for the sick, suffering, and dying.
>
> *Closing Prayer:* Dear Jesus, please increase our faith.
>
> *All pray the Our Father, Hail Mary, and Glory Be.*
>
> *All through the Day:* God wants me to give my heart to him.

THURSDAY, FIFTH WEEK OF LENT

Have you thought about the talents that God has given you? Have you thought of how you can put them at the service of others? Do not bury your talents! Set your stakes on great ideals, the ideals that enlarge the heart, the ideals of service that make your talents fruitful.

—*General Audience, April 24, 2013*

Parent Reflection

Each of our children possesses many gifts from God. They might not realize it but it's true. Each one is blessed with their own unique gifts. Throughout life, they will start to discover them and unearth them to use to serve others. Parents have the unique and significant mission of helping their children discover and embrace their gifts, as well as encouraging them to use them for God's glory. Ponder ways to talk to your kids about their gifts and how they might use them to help others.

Family Prayer

All make the Sign of the Cross.

> *Parent:* Dear Jesus, thank you for the many blessings you bestow upon us. Please forgive us for our selfishness at times.

> Now let us listen to these words of Pope Francis.

A parent or child now reads the opening quotation aloud.

> *All:* Blessed Mother Mary, bring us closer to your Son, Jesus.

A Story from Pope Francis's Life

Pope Francis continued to live a frugal life as the pope. He often raised awareness of those we are called to serve. He didn't mince words when he said, "How can it be that it's not a news item when an elderly homeless person dies of exposure, but it is news when the stock market loses two points? This is a clear case of exclusion!" (*The Joy of the Gospel*, par. 53).

Fasting

Today, fast from selfishness. When tempted to do something for yourself, try to give something to another instead (even if giving is only a simple smile).

Almsgiving

Give a surprise gift of helping with a chore, giving a kind compliment or gesture.

Prayer

> *Today's Intention:* Let's pray for the homeless and unfortunate.
>
> *Closing Prayer:* Dear Jesus, help us to work harder at giving of ourselves and using our gifts.
>
> *All pray the Our Father, Hail Mary, and Glory Be.*
>
> *All through the Day:* God has given us many gifts to use for others.

FRIDAY, FIFTH WEEK OF LENT

Jesus Christ did not save us with an idea, or an intellectual program. He saved us with his flesh, with the concreteness of the flesh. He lowered himself, became man, and was made flesh until the end.

—Homily, Domus Sanctae Marthae, June 14, 2013

Parent Reflection

This is a very good day to schedule Confession for your family, either this weekend or during Holy Week, which is fast approaching. Talk to the kids about the fact that, as Pope Francis points out above, Jesus humbled himself during his life even though he was God. He gave his life so that we may have Eternal Life. Ask the kids to think about that today and to share their thoughts about it when you come together.

Family Prayer

All make the Sign of the Cross.

Parent: Dear Jesus, thank you for loving us so much that you gave your life for us.

Now let us listen to these words of Pope Francis.

A parent or child now reads the opening quotation aloud.

All: Blessed Mother Mary, bring us closer to your Son, Jesus.

A Story from Pope Francis's Life

Pope Francis was one to get into the trenches of life, not fearing poor conditions, illness, and strife. He wanted to come face to face with life so he could minister to the needs of the people—to show them Christ's love. He also spoke of the importance and blessing in praying for those who are not particularly nice to us or who bother us in some way. In *The Joy of the Gospel*, he said, "To pray for someone whom I am irritated is a beautiful step forward in love and an act of evangelization. Do this today! Let us not allow ourselves to be robbed of the ideal of fraternal love!" (par. 101).

Fasting

Today, fast from complaining. When tempted, instead say, "I love you, Jesus!"

Almsgiving

Take time to thank Jesus for his great love for your family. Plan a way as a family to show God's love by helping someone in need.

Prayer

Today's Intention: Let's pray for persecuted and tortured people around the world.

Closing Prayer: Dear Jesus, thank you for blessing us with our faith in you.

All pray the Our Father, Hail Mary, and Glory Be.

All through the Day: I will try to be mindful of the needs of others rather than focusing on myself.

PASSION (PALM) SUNDAY

Holy Week is a good occasion to go to confession and to take up the right path again.

—*Twitter, April 14, 2014*

Parent Reflection

Today is Passion Sunday (or Palm Sunday). It is the last Sunday in our Lenten journey. We can recall its significance in salvation history. Today's feast commemorates Jesus' triumphant entry into Jerusalem to celebrate the Passover. People rushed over to see Jesus, considering him to be their king. They laid out palm branches before him as he rode in on a donkey fulfilling the prophecy of Zechariah: "See your king shall come to you; a just savior is he, meek, and riding on an ass, on a colt, the foal of an ass"(Zec 9:9). They called out, "Hosanna to the Son of David; Blessed is he who comes in the name of the Lord! Hosanna in the highest heaven!" (Mt 21:9).

We observe much symbolism. The donkey symbolized peace. The palm branches signified that a dignitary or king was arriving in glory and triumph. Through the ages, palm branches have been used in procession on Palm Sunday and represent joy and victory. The faithful take them and use them in their homes as sacramentals—sometimes thrown into a fire during storms, placed on graves, in fields, and barns. Ashes from burned palms are used for the following Ash Wednesday's ashes.

Holy Week begins today with the reading of the Passion at Mass. We should strive to meditate on the events of the Passion throughout the coming week. This is truly the holiest of weeks and there are many graces for the asking.

Family Prayer

All make the Sign of the Cross.

> *Parent:* Dear Jesus, we are sorry for the times we haven't listened to you.

Now let us listen to these words of Pope Francis.

A parent or child now reads the opening quotation aloud.

All: Blessed Mother Mary, bring us closer to your Son, Jesus.

A Story from Pope Francis's Life

When Pope Francis was asked to describe himself in a 2013 interview, he perhaps surprised the interviewer when he said, "I am a sinner." The pontiff didn't go into his background or family history; he simply said he was a sinner. "This is the most accurate definition. It is not a figure of speech, a literary genre. I am a sinner."

During that same interview, Pope Francis referred to a famous painting by Caravaggio known as *The Calling of St. Matthew*. It was on the feast of Saint Matthew in 1953 when Pope Francis felt a calling to religious life. The painting depicts a pivotal moment in Matthew's life—Jesus enters the tax collector's lair, finds Matthew, and singles him out by pointing to him. Matthew holds onto his money and seems to say, "No, not me!"

Relating to Saint Matthew's reaction at that momentous time in his life, Pope Francis said, "It is the gesture of Matthew that strikes me. . . . And this is what I said when they asked me if I would accept my election as pontiff . . . 'I am a sinner, but I trust in the infinite mercy and patience of our Lord Jesus Christ, and I accept in a spirit of penance.'"[2]

Fasting

Today, fast from being upset with someone. Instead of feeling angry or upset, forgive them in your heart.

Almsgiving

Take time today to think about those who have hurt you in some way. Do you forgive them? Now is the time. Forgive them. If possible, tell them. Pray for them.

Prayer

Today's Intention: Let's forgive and pray for all who have harmed us in some way.

Closing Prayer: Dear Jesus, forgive us of our sins. Grant us the graces to be more loving and forgiving.

All pray the Our Father, Hail Mary, and Glory Be.

All through the Day: Jesus wants me to be loving and forgiving.

Let us also remember Peter: three times he denied Jesus, precisely when he should have been closest to him; and when he hits bottom, he meets the gaze of Jesus, who patiently, wordlessly, says to him, "Peter, don't be afraid of your weakness; trust in me." Peter understands, he feels the loving gaze of Jesus and he weeps.

How beautiful is this gaze of Jesus—how much tenderness is there! Brothers and sisters, let us never lose trust in the patience and mercy of God!

—*Homily, Divine Mercy Sunday, April 7, 2013*

Parent Reflection

The saints are a constant reminder of our weaknesses and human frailty but also of our strengths. They were human like us and needed to be steadfast in their faith and in their prayer lives to move forward toward heaven. We, too, are called to be saints. Mother Teresa often proclaimed, "Holiness is not the luxury of a few, but a simple duty for you and me." She was not implying that it was an easy task to follow God, but that we are all required to be saints. She also said, "I will, I want, with God's blessing, to be holy."[3]

Pope Francis reminds us in his words above that even St. Peter failed. We all fail at times. But let's keep our gaze always on Jesus and allow him to gaze upon us—to transform us!

On a practical note, try to do any Easter shopping earlier this week rather than later during the holy days of the Triduum.

Family Prayer

All make the Sign of the Cross.

Parent: Dear Jesus, help me to answer your call to holiness.

Now let us listen to these words of Pope Francis.

A parent or child now reads the opening quotation aloud.

All: Blessed Mother Mary, bring us closer to your Son, Jesus.

A Story from Pope Francis's Life

Pope Francis challenges everyone to serve the poor and needy and not make excuses as to why we cannot. He specifically tells us, "No one must say that they cannot be close to the poor because their own lifestyle demands more attention to other areas" (*The Joy of the Gospel*, par. 201). Naturally, serving the poor takes on a myriad of forms for all of us in our various walks of life. But Pope Francis continues to encourage us to encounter the poor—to come face to face with them whenever possible. That is where God will be working in our hearts and in their hearts.

Fasting

Today, fast from any quarreling. Encourage everyone to be virtuous. When tempted to argue, pause and offer a kind word instead.

Almsgiving

Ask the children to consider how they might be an instrument of God's peace today.

Prayer

Today's Intention: Let's pray for peace in the world.

Closing Prayer: Dear Jesus, help us each to be an instrument of peace, starting in our domestic church.

All pray the Our Father, Hail Mary, and Glory Be.

All through the Day: God calls me to become holy.

TUESDAY OF HOLY WEEK

In Holy Week, we live the crowning moment of this journey, of this plan of love that runs through the entire history of the relations between God and humanity. Jesus enters Jerusalem to take his last step with which he sums up the whole of his existence. He gives himself without reserve; he keeps nothing for himself, not even life.

—*General Audience, March 27, 2013*

Parent Reflection

We are making our way through Holy Week already. We may lament that this Lenten journey has not been what we had expected. But if we trust God and allow him to work in our lives, we come to realize that he is in control—not us. All of the extra challenges are actually opportunities for grace, depending upon how we respond to them. Let's make this Holy Week really count. Let's make extra efforts to partake in whatever parish services we can and to impress upon the children the enormity of this Holy Week. Graces abound. We should ask for them.

Family Prayer

All make the Sign of the Cross.

Parent: Dear Jesus, bring us closer to you this Holy Week.

Now let us listen to these words of Pope Francis.

A parent or child now reads the opening quotation aloud.

All: Blessed Mother Mary, bring us closer to your Son, Jesus.

A Story from Pope Francis's Life

Pope Francis inspires the faithful to be evangelizers in their own walks of life. Rather than become discouraged about our darkened world,

Pope Francis pushes us forth to have confidence in God. He said, "God is able to act in every situation."

There will always be difficulties, setbacks, dark times, and intense struggles, but "goodness always re-emerges and spreads," he reminds us. We have to hang onto the hope that Christ's resurrection has triumphed and will triumph over all evil in the end "Such is the power of the resurrection, and all who evangelize are instruments of that power," he said (*The Joy of the Gospel*, par. 276).

Fasting

Today, fast from expecting (wanting things to go a certain way, etc.). Instead, trust God with everything today.

Almsgiving

Give your heart totally to God. Take at least ten minutes' time in quiet prayer to tell him about it.

Prayer

Today's Intention: Let's pray for families everywhere.

Closing Prayer: Dear Jesus, protect families all over the world. Help our family be a light to others.

All pray the Our Father, Hail Mary, and Glory Be.

All through the Day: God loves me with a deep and everlasting love.

But the Cross of Christ invites us also to allow ourselves to be smitten by his love, teaching us always to look upon others with mercy and tenderness, especially those who suffer, who are in need of help, who need a word or a concrete action. . . . How many times have we seen them in the Way of the Cross, how many times have they accompanied Jesus on the way to Calvary: Pilate, Simon of Cyrene, Mary, the women. . . .

And you, who do you want to be? Like Pilate? Like Simon? Like Mary? Jesus is looking at you now and is asking you: Do you want to help me carry the Cross? Brothers and sisters . . . how will you respond to him?

—*Address, World Youth Day, Way of the Cross, July 26, 2013*

Parent Reflection

A mid the tremendous joys we feel in our hearts as parents raising our children closer to heaven, we also experience sufferings and pain in our persevering role. We can offer everything to Jesus and ask him if we can, in a sense, accompany him on the way of Calvary as Pope Francis suggests. Take time today to ponder what that might be. Reflect upon who you want to be like. Are you like Pilate as Pope Francis asks? Or do you strive to be like Simon of Cyrene or Mary? What can you do to show Our Lord that you will walk with him and that you will help to carry the Cross?

Family Prayer

All make the Sign of the Cross.

Parent: Dear Jesus, open our hearts to all of the graces you wish to bestow on our family this Holy Week.

Now let us listen to these words of Pope Francis.

A parent or child now reads the opening quotation aloud.

All: Blessed Mother Mary, bring us closer to your Son, Jesus.

A Story from Pope Francis's Life

Pope Francis challenges us in his words above about Jesus' passion and death on the cross, asking us how we will respond. Throughout his papacy, he also encourages the faithful with the reminder of the miraculous power in Jesus' resurrection, pushing us forth to evangelize according to how the Lord is calling us. Pope Francis reassures us that faithful evangelizers are instruments of the resurrection, walking alongside Christ. He said, "Christ's resurrection everywhere calls forth seeds of that new world; even if they are cut back, they grow again, for the resurrection is already secretly woven into the fabric of this history, for Jesus did not rise in vain" (*The Joy of the Gospel*, par. 278).

Fasting

Today, fast from idle gossip. If you are tempted to talk about another, compliment them, speak well of them, or don't speak about them at all.

Almsgiving

Encourage the children to make a card, draw a picture, or write an uplifting verse to be given to someone on Easter Sunday.

Prayer

Today's Intention: Let's pray for all missionaries.

Closing Prayer: Dear Jesus, help me to offer my whole life to you.

All pray the Our Father, Hail Mary, and Glory Be.

All through the Day: By offering loving sacrifices and prayers, I can help save souls by God's grace.

At the Last Supper with his friends, he breaks the bread and passes the cup round "for us." The Son of God offers himself to us; he puts his Body and his Blood into our hands, so as to be with us always, to dwell among us.

—*General Audience, March 27, 2013*

Parent Reflection

Today, we commemorate the Last Supper and the institution of the Eucharist as well as the priesthood. Talk to the children about observing this holy day with a humble and prayerful heart. Tell them about the great sacraments that were instituted on this day about two thousand years ago including Holy Orders, which has blessed us with priests, and the Eucharist, which gives us life. Consider asking Mother Mary and your guardian angels to accompany you throughout the Holy Triduum, the next few holy days leading up to Easter Sunday.

Family Prayer

All make the Sign of the Cross.

Parent: Dear Jesus, help us to reverently observe the holiness of this great day.

Now let us listen to these words of Pope Francis.

A parent or child now reads the opening quotation aloud.

All: Blessed Mother Mary, bring us closer to your Son, Jesus.

A Story from Pope Francis's Life

Many believe that Pope Francis caused quite an uproar in interviews he gave in the fall of 2013. His comments seemed controversial. Pope Francis's vision for the Church is to go out to meet others instead of merely opening the doors of the Church and expecting them to come in. He wants the world to know about the healing and saving power of Jesus' love. Pope Francis described the Church as a field hospital for the suffering. He said, "The thing the church needs most today is the ability to heal wounds and to warm the hearts of the faithful; it needs nearness, proximity." He explained in one interview that when ministering to the seriously wounded we don't focus on other issues—we take care of their most serious wounds first. "Then we can talk about everything else." He continued, "We cannot insist only on issues related to abortion, gay marriage, and contraceptive methods," explaining that "it is not necessary to talk about these issues all the time."[4]

Fasting

Today, fast from technology as much as possible. Try to keep a quiet atmosphere in an effort to be more prayerful. Help one another. Show Christ's love.

Almsgiving

Give more time for prayer and spiritual reading today.

Prayer

Today's Intention: Let's pray for priests.

Closing Prayer: Dear Jesus, we love you. Please help us to fully open our hearts to you.

All pray the Our Father, Hail Mary, and Glory Be.

All through the Day: God wants me to be prayerful today.

GOOD FRIDAY

Jesus gave himself up to death voluntarily in order to reciprocate the love of God the Father, in perfect union with his will, to demonstrate his love for us. On the Cross, Jesus "loved me and gave himself for me." Each one can say this "for me."

—*General Audience, March 27, 2013*

Parent Reflection

Today is one of the most significant days on our Church calendar. We commemorate the day that Jesus was tortured, suffered, and was put to death on a cross for all of us—"to demonstrate his love for us." What a great mystery lies within the Cross of Jesus! Try your best to schedule your family's day so that you can attend church services and also observe a very quiet and prayerful tone in the household. Encourage the family to offer up any sufferings or sickness to God, praying that they can be united with Christ's passion. Ponder ways you might make sacrifices today without grumbling or complaining, striving to please God and help others. Consider how Mother Mary faithfully stayed with her son until the end, offering prayers and love. What can you learn from her?

Family Prayer

All make the Sign of the Cross.

Parent: Dear Jesus, I give you my heart.

Now let us listen to these words of Pope Francis.

A parent or child now reads the opening quotation aloud.

All: Blessed Mother Mary, bring us closer to your Son, Jesus.

A Story from Pope Francis's Life

The day following the interview in 2013 in which he made statements that were considered controversial, Pope Francis spoke out in defense of human life. He addressed a group of Catholic gynecologists and said that human life "is sacred—at each phase and at every age . . . it is always valuable. And not as a matter of faith—no, no—but of reason, as a matter of science!" He vehemently condemned abortion, stating that it was a result of a "widespread mentality of the useful, the 'culture of waste' that asks for the elimination of human beings, especially if they are physically or socially weaker. Our response to this mentality is a decisive and unhesitating 'yes' to life."[5]

Fasting

Follow the fasting rules for Good Friday noted in the introduction to this book. Take time today to pray the "Prayer to Our Lady, Undoer of Knots" at the end of this book.

Almsgiving

Is there an act of charity you can do as a family today to help a relative or neighbor?

Prayer

> *Today's Intention:* Let's pray for prisoners and the persecuted of the world. Ask St. Dismas, the good thief who hung alongside of Jesus, to intercede for conversions.
>
> *Closing Prayer:* Dear Jesus, I can never thank you enough for dying for me.
>
> *All pray the Our Father, Hail Mary, and Glory Be.*
>
> *All through the Day:* I am blessed to be a Christian Catholic.

HOLY SATURDAY

The logic of the Cross . . . is not primarily that of suffering and death, but rather that of love and of the gift of self which brings life. . . . Following and accompanying Christ, staying with him, demands "coming out of ourselves," requires us to be outgoing: to come out of ourselves, out of a dreary way of living faith that has become a habit, out of the temptation to withdraw into our own plans, which end by shutting out God's creative action.

—General Audience, March 27, 2013

Parent Reflection

Holy Saturday is a day to remember that Jesus was crucified and then sealed away in the tomb. Churches are stripped bare of everything and there's a quiet sadness that fills our hearts when we have prayerfully entered into the Holy Triduum. We should reflect upon what the disciples might have felt, missing their Messiah. Being alone and afraid, they hid in the upper room with the Blessed Mother, praying earnestly to the Holy Spirit to come to them. After all, Jesus had promised them.

Look for times of silence and prayer today and encourage the family to think of Jesus and to thank him for his great love for us. Now is the time to prepare your hearts in great hope for the Resurrection.

Family Prayer

All make the Sign of the Cross.

> *Parent:* Dear Jesus, you suffered and died a cruel death for me. Open my heart fully to your love.

Now let us listen to these words of Pope Francis.

A parent or child now reads the opening quotation aloud.

> *All:* Blessed Mother Mary, bring us closer to your Son, Jesus.

A Story from Pope Francis's Life

The Blessed Mother is beloved to Pope Francis. She is our reliable guide toward heaven. Mary's "yes" to God in her *fiat* at the Annunciation and her continued renewed "yes" throughout her life encourages others along the way. She pondered, prayed, and kept up that vital conversation with God. Mary continues to inspire the faithful in our own day to press on throughout trials, persecution, and uncertainty. Mary was a faithful disciple of Jesus, persevering to the bitter end.

Pope Francis tells us that Mary is indeed the "star of the New Evangelization." He asks her to "help us to bear radiant witness to communion, service, ardent and generous faith, justice, and love of the poor, that the joy of the Gospel may reach to the ends of the earth, illuminating even the fringes of our world" (*The Joy of the Gospel*, par. 288).

Fasting

Today, fast from popular culture as best as you can (television, magazines, Internet, shopping malls, radio, etc.).

Almsgiving

Give time to Jesus in thanksgiving today. Think of a way to show his love to others in need.

Prayer

Today's Intention: Let's pray for families everywhere, especially those who do not believe in God.

Closing Prayer: Dear Jesus, help us to spread your love everywhere we go.

All pray the Our Father, Hail Mary, and Glory Be.

All through the Day: I am so blessed to be a Catholic!

EASTER SUNDAY

At dawn, they went to the tomb to anoint Jesus' body and found the first sign: the empty tomb. Their meeting with a messenger of God followed. He announced: "Jesus of Nazareth, the Crucified One, has risen, he is not here" (cf. Mk 16:1, 5–6). The women were motivated by love and were able to accept this announcement with faith: they believed and passed it on straight away; they did not keep it to themselves but passed it on. . . .

This should happen in our lives, too. Let us feel the joy of being Christian! We believe in the Risen One who conquered evil and death! Let us have the courage to "come out of ourselves" to take this joy and this light to all the places of our life!

—*General Audience, April 3, 2013*

Parent Reflection

Christ the Lord is risen today! Alleluia! Happy Easter! This is a day of profound celebration. Jesus' rising from the dead has given us the promise of new life in this life and in the next. Enjoy this feast of all feasts—be blessed at holy Mass and celebrate fully with your family—bask in the joy of Easter! Carry the holy joy into the days ahead, hanging onto Easter hope, always lighting the way for others.

Family Prayer

All make the Sign of the Cross.

Parent: Dear Jesus, I love you! Thank you for loving me!

Now let us listen to these words of Pope Francis.

A parent or child now reads the opening quotation aloud.

All: Blessed Mother Mary, bring us closer to your Son, Jesus.

A Story from Pope Francis's Life

In his encyclical letter *The Light of Faith*, Pope Francis said, "There is an urgent need, then, to see once again that faith is a light, for once the flame of faith dies out, all other lights begin to dim. The light of faith is unique, since it is capable of illuminating *every aspect* of human existence. A light this powerful cannot come from ourselves but from a more primordial source: in a word, it must come from God" (par. 04).

These are beautiful thoughts to ponder. Let's be sure to allow the light of faith to live in us, guide us, and radiate from us—always!

Fasting

Today is a day to celebrate so no fasting is necessary. However, encourage the whole family to retain the spirit of prayer that was fostered in their hearts throughout the holy season of Lent. God will certainly be very pleased with their continual sacrifices, prayers, and acts of love offered to him in love.

Almsgiving

Give to one another today and enjoy the beautiful feast of Easter!

Prayer

Today's Intention: Let's pray for the Church, all its members, and all the hierarchy. Let us continue to pray that others will convert and come into the Church.

Closing Prayer: Dear Jesus, help me to be a radiant light to others.

All pray the Our Father, Hail Mary, and Glory Be.

All through the Day: Jesus has risen! Alleluia!

Jesus makes himself present in a new way; he is the Crucified One, but his body is glorified; he did not return to earthly life but returned in a new condition. . . . For us, too, there are many signs through which the Risen One makes himself known: Sacred Scripture, the Eucharist, the other sacraments, charity, all those acts of love which bring a ray of the Risen One. Let us permit ourselves to be illuminated by Christ's resurrection, let him transform us with his power, so that through us, too, the signs of death may give way to signs of life in the world.

—*General Audience, April 3, 2013*

Carry your Easter joy throughout the days ahead. May God bless you and your family!

PRAYER TO OUR LADY, UNDOER OF KNOTS

M ary, Undoer of Knots, pray for us.
Through your grace,
your intercession,
and your example,
deliver us from all evil,
Our Lady, and untie the knots
that prevent us from being
united with God,
so that we, free from sin and error,
may find him in all things,
may have our hearts placed in him,
and may serve him always
in our brothers and sisters.
Amen.

Prayer written by Pope Francis, inspired by the painting *Mary, Undoer of Knots.*

Pray these prayers for the Holy Father's intentions: Our Father, Hail Mary, and Glory Be.

NOTES

1. "Pope Francis: Lent Is a Time to Adjust Your Life," *en.radiovaticana.va*, March 18, 2014, accessed April 28, 2015, http://en.radiovaticana.va/storico/2014/03/18/pope_francis_lent_a_time_to_adjust_your_life/en1-782518.

2. Anthony Spadaro, S.J., "A Big Heart Open to God: The Exclusive Interview with Pope Francis," *America*, September 30, 2013.

3. Mother Teresa, *Where There Is Love, There Is God*, edited and with an introduction by Brian Kolodiejchuk, M.C. (New York: Doubleday, 2010), 344.

4. Spadaro, "A Big Heart Open to God."

5. Pope Francis, "Address to Participants in the Meeting Organized by the International Federation of Catholic Medical Associations," *www.vatican.va*, September 20, 2013.

ABOUT THE AUTHOR

Donna-Marie Cooper O'Boyle is an award-winning and best-selling author and journalist, speaker, pilgrimage host, retreat leader, and the EWTN television host of *Everyday Blessings for Catholic Moms* and *Catholic Mom's Café*, which she created. A Catholic wife and mother of five, Cooper O'Boyle was noted as one of the Top Ten Most Fascinating Catholics in 2009 by *Faith & Family Live*. She enjoyed a decade-long friendship with Blessed Mother Teresa of Calcutta and became a Lay Missionary of Charity. For many years her spiritual director was Servant of God John A. Hardon, S.J., who also served as one of Mother Teresa's spiritual directors.

Cooper O'Boyle was invited by the Holy See in 2008 to participate in an international congress for women at the Vatican to mark the twentieth anniversary of the apostolic letter *Mulieris Dignitatem* (On the Dignity and Vocation of Women). She received apostolic blessings from Saint John Paul II and Pope Benedict XVI on her books and work and a special blessing from Saint John Paul II for her work with Blessed Mother Teresa. Cooper O'Boyle is the author of twenty books on faith and family, including *Rooted in Love*, *The Miraculous Medal*, *Mother Teresa and Me*, *Catholic Mom's Café*, and *The Kiss of Jesus*. She has been featured by Zenit news, *Vatican Insider*, and *Rome Reports* and is a frequent guest on *EWTN Bookmark*, *Sunday Night Prime*, and *Women of Grace*. She maintains several blogs and her website donnacooperoboyle.com